GW00601938

For further information
about Action Books, please write to:

Barrie & Jenkins Ltd.,
24 Highbury Crescent,
London N5 1RX

BOOKS

© Chancerel 1976
© Chancerel Publishers 1977

English language edition

All rights reserved. No part of this publication may be
reproduced, recorded, transmitted or stored
in any retrieval system, in any form whatsoever,
without the written permission of the copyright holder.

This edition is not for sale in the USA.

Chancerel Publishers Ltd.,
40 Tavistock Street,
London WC2E 7PB

ISBN-0-905703-13-8

Photoset by Tottenham Typesetters, London
Printed in Italy.

GOLF
100 ways to improve your game

TENNIS
Basic techniques and tactics

PHOTOGRAPHY
Using a 35 mm camera

YOGA
The happy way to live

JUDO
The practical way

MOTORCYCLES
Maintain your own machine

SWIMMING
Learning, training, competing

MOTORCARS
Maintenance and minor repairs

HOME MOVIES
Make and project your own films

COOKERY
Skills of French cuisine

FREEZING
Save time, money and eat well

BASKETBALL
Scoring skills and strategies

CHESS
Master the moves

WOODWORKING
Tools, techniques and projects

KNITTING
Patterns, stitches and styles

KNITTING

Patterns, stitches and styles

Maureen Briggs

Drawings by Max Lenvers

Chancerel | BARRIE & JENKINS
COMMUNICA-EUROPA

75p

In 1975 a red-headed Yorkshire girl sprang to fame from the television screen and the Grand Final of the talent-spotting show, 'New Faces'. She was Marti Caine, orphan, teenage model, wife and mother of two boys and now an international variety star. At sixteen she appeared in several major magazines, modelling fashions. At seventeen she married. But what she really wanted to do was sing. The trouble was that people laughed. They laughed her into realising that her true calling was comedy – with the result that she has had two television series in Britain already, with numerous guest appearances. She has played in Las Vegas (to great acclaim) and in future her programme looks like taking her to South Africa, the Middle East, Australia and Japan. Knitting is a hobby she took up young – at school in fact. Ever since then she has knitted keenly, but with varying success. 'The first things I knitted for the boys,' she remembers, 'were nylon wool sweaters that stretched and stretched, so they grew up with their owners.' But she still hasn't worn any of her home knitted clothes on stage. 'One tends to look better in evening dress,' she says.

The bigger the needles and the chunkier the wool, the better – I'm that impatient when I knit. I learned to knit at school in Scotland, where you need every sweater you can get in winter. Then later I used to keep the whole family in sweaters. But time seems to be at a premium these days. And even though I knit while waiting to go on stage – it's a great way to relax – it can take me weeks to make something a normal knitter makes in hours. Still, I love the feeling of achievement and satisfaction knitting gives me, especially when the patterns are in smart, chunky styles like many in this book. And if I were learning from these illustrations, perhaps I'd be able to knit faster – or with smaller needles!

Marti Caine

MARTI CAINE

KNITTING KNOW-HOW 9
Knitting equipment 10
All summed up 10
Look up the terms 11
Visiting the woolshop 11

SNUG SCARVES 21
Materials 22
Spider stitch 22
Joining in a new ball of wool 23
Casting off stitches 23
Casting off the last stitch 24
Making a fringe 24
Attaching the fringe 25
Scarf variations 25

STRIPY SWEATERS 35
Materials 36
Casting on – the thumb method 36
Moss stitch 37
How to hold the yarn 37
Knitting in stripes 39
The front 39
Casting on extra stitches 40
Shaping the slash neckline 40
The back 41
Completing the sweater and variations 41

TRY IT FOR TENSION 13
Why knit tension squares? 14
What you need 14
Simple casting on 16
Plain stitch 16
Holding the needle – a row 17
Counting stitches – garter stitch 17
Measuring the tension square 19
Checking the tension 19

TANK TOPS 27
Materials 28
Measurements 28
Stocking stitch 29
Purl stitch 29
The borders 30
The side edges and the back 30
The front 32
Invisible seams 32
Oversewing 33
Tank top variations 33

WOOLLY WAISTCOATS 43
Materials 44
Rice stitch 44
Slipping a stitch 46
Shaping 46
Shaping – back and front 47
Simple decreasing 47
Slip decreasing 49
Completing the waistcoat and variations 49

Contents

**STOCKING STITCH
SWEATERS** 51
Materials 52
Lace stitch band 52
Chain edge 53
Making a hem 53
Picking up stitches 54
The sleeves 54
Making the drawstring 55
Completing the sweater 55

HUSKY POLO NECKS 65
Materials 66
Two and two ribbing 66
The sleeves 67
Fair-Isle pattern 67
Fair-Isle – watch the colours 68
Sleeve decreasings 68
The back and front 70
The neckband 70
Completion and invisible seams 71
Fair-Isle variations 71

**PICK UP HINTS AND
DROPPED STITCHES** 81
Which way am I knitting? 82
Casting off too tightly 82
Picking up a dropped stitch
(plain) 83
Picking up a dropped stitch
(purl) 83
Untwisting stitches 85
Undoing stitches and rows 85
Sewing on neck edgings and
borders 86
Knitting two pieces alike 86
Adding a buttonhole 87
Adding at patch pocket 87

CHUNKY CABLE SWEATERS 57
Materials 58
Cable pattern 58
Beaded edge 59
The sleeves 59
The back 60
The front 60
Knitting the shoulder seams
together 62
The neckband 62
Knitting in rounds 63

JAUNTY JACKETS 73
Materials 74
The back 74
Sloping the shoulders 75
Slit pockets 75
The fronts 76
Increasing in the middle of a
row 76
The sleeves 78
Front borders 78
The buttonholes 79
Borders for neck and pockets 79

**GLOSSARY AND
ABBREVIATIONS** 88

KNITTING KNOWLEDGE 89

SIZES OF KNITTING NEEDLES 89

BIOGRAPHY 90

PHOTOGRAPHS 91

Knitting know-how

You want to learn to knit? Then, this is where you start.
Follow the illustrations and diagrams; they will enable you to master the basic techniques of knitting in no time at all. Then as you progress you'll find there's a pattern to suit your knitting standard, from a simple chunky scarf to a super tweed jacket. But be sure to read this chapter before you pick up your needles. It will start you off in the right direction.

Knitting equipment

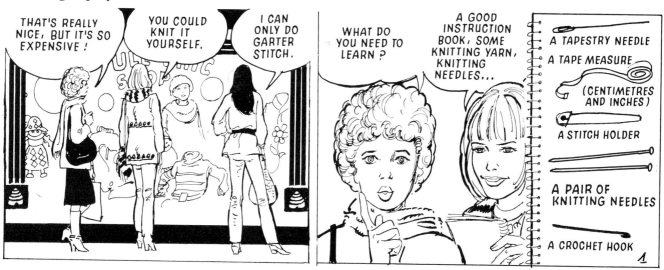

All summed up

Look up the terms

Visiting the woolshop

Try it for tension

You don't want to waste time and money carefully following a knitting
pattern and then having to give the finished result to your little sister,
because the garment is too small for you. So, always knit a tension square
before you start the actual pattern. It's a small test piece which allows
you to try the stitch and to check that the tension of your knitting
corresponds to that of the pattern.

Why knit tension squares?

I'M GOING TO START WITH A SMALL TENSION SQUARE TO TRY OUT THE PATTERN.

I'M NOT. I ALREADY KNOW HOW TO DO THIS STITCH.

YES, YOU TOO, ANNE. YOU SHOULD ALWAYS KNIT A TEST SQUARE TO CHECK YOUR TENSION. THE SQUARE SHOULD BE AT LEAST 13 x 13 cms OR 5 x 5 ins, TO BE SURE YOU DON'T MAKE ANY MISTAKES WHEN COUNTING THE STITCHES.

5

What you need

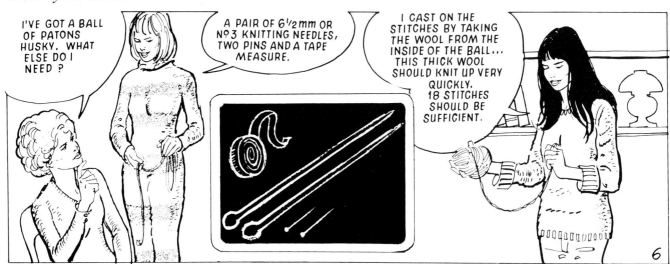

I'VE GOT A BALL OF PATONS HUSKY. WHAT ELSE DO I NEED?

A PAIR OF 6½ mm OR №3 KNITTING NEEDLES, TWO PINS AND A TAPE MEASURE.

I CAST ON THE STITCHES BY TAKING THE WOOL FROM THE INSIDE OF THE BALL... THIS THICK WOOL SHOULD KNIT UP VERY QUICKLY. 18 STITCHES SHOULD BE SUFFICIENT.

6

Simple casting on

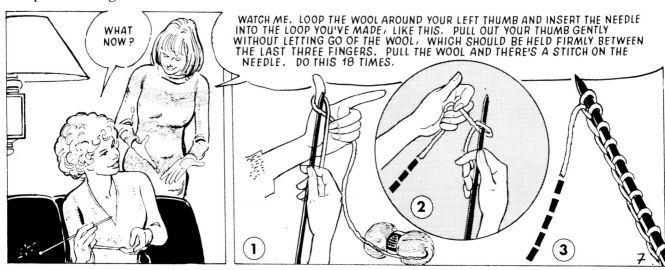

WHAT NOW?

WATCH ME. LOOP THE WOOL AROUND YOUR LEFT THUMB AND INSERT THE NEEDLE INTO THE LOOP YOU'VE MADE, LIKE THIS. PULL OUT YOUR THUMB GENTLY WITHOUT LETTING GO OF THE WOOL, WHICH SHOULD BE HELD FIRMLY BETWEEN THE LAST THREE FINGERS. PULL THE WOOL AND THERE'S A STITCH ON THE NEEDLE. DO THIS 18 TIMES.

Plain stitch

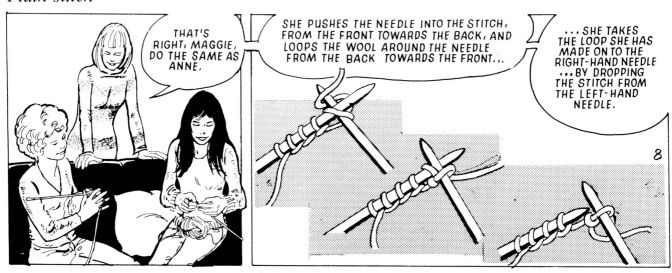

THAT'S RIGHT, MAGGIE, DO THE SAME AS ANNE.

SHE PUSHES THE NEEDLE INTO THE STITCH, FROM THE FRONT TOWARDS THE BACK, AND LOOPS THE WOOL AROUND THE NEEDLE FROM THE BACK TOWARDS THE FRONT...

...SHE TAKES THE LOOP SHE HAS MADE ON TO THE RIGHT-HAND NEEDLE ...BY DROPPING THE STITCH FROM THE LEFT-HAND NEEDLE.

Holding the needle – a row

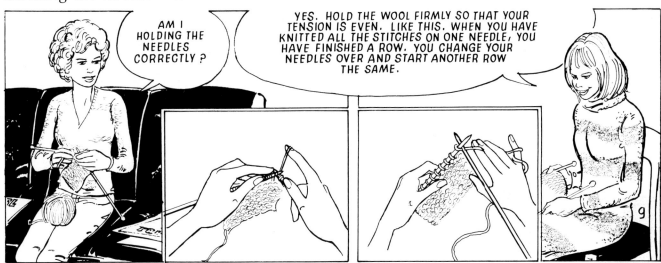

Counting stitches – garter stitch

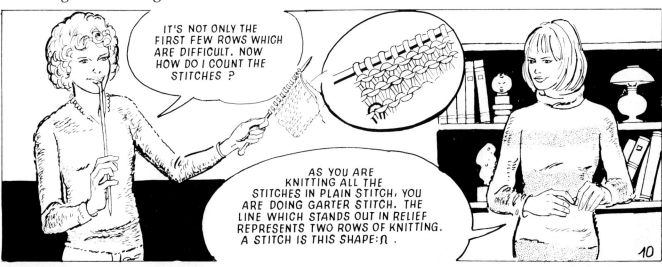

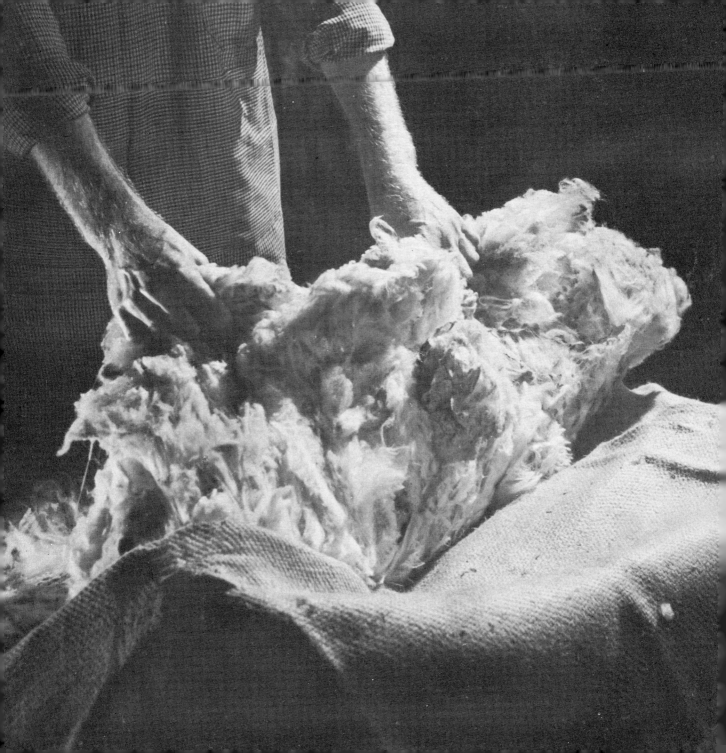

Measuring the tension square

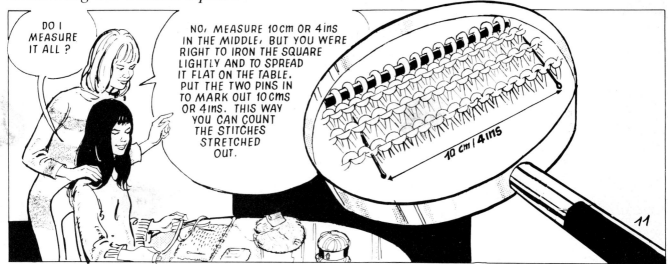

Checking the tension

Snug scarves

By all means be ambitious – but don't over-reach yourself. Start with
something simple – knit a scarf! It's the ideal beginner's project. You
don't need much patience or experience to make it. Just 300 grammes of
wool and a little of your spare time. Try knitting it in red, or natural, or
in three or four colours. It'll look really smart.

Materials

Spider stitch

Joining in a new ball of wool

14 STITCHES TO 10 CMS OR 4 INS, MY TENSION IS OK. I'LL CAST ON 26 STITCHES AND CARRY ON KNITTING.

I'M FASTER THAN YOU. I'VE CAST ON 26 STITCHES AND USED UP MY FIRST BALL OF WOOL.

THREAD THE END OF THE NEW BALL INTO THE TAPESTRY NEEDLE AND THEN THREAD IT THROUGH THE END OF THE BALL WHICH IS RUNNING OUT.

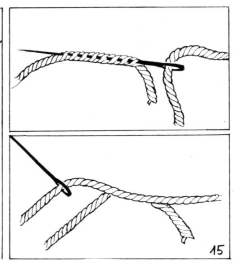

15

Casting off stitches

I'VE KNITTED ABOUT TWO METRES OR SIX FEET, IS THAT ENOUGH ?

IT'S GREAT.

ALL YOU HAVE TO DO NOW IS CAST OFF ...

16

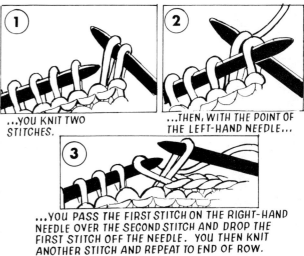

① ...YOU KNIT TWO STITCHES.

② ...THEN, WITH THE POINT OF THE LEFT-HAND NEEDLE...

③ ...YOU PASS THE FIRST STITCH ON THE RIGHT-HAND NEEDLE OVER THE SECOND STITCH AND DROP THE FIRST STITCH OFF THE NEEDLE. YOU THEN KNIT ANOTHER STITCH AND REPEAT TO END OF ROW.

Casting off the last stitch

Making a fringe

Attaching the fringe

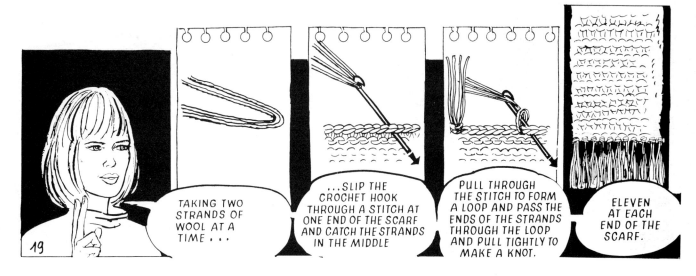

TAKING TWO STRANDS OF WOOL AT A TIME...

...SLIP THE CROCHET HOOK THROUGH A STITCH AT ONE END OF THE SCARF AND CATCH THE STRANDS IN THE MIDDLE

PULL THROUGH THE STITCH TO FORM A LOOP AND PASS THE ENDS OF THE STRANDS THROUGH THE LOOP AND PULL TIGHTLY TO MAKE A KNOT.

ELEVEN AT EACH END OF THE SCARF.

Scarf variations

WE CAN DO A LOT OF THINGS NOW.

ONLY USING GARTER STITCH?

...BLANKETS, PONCHOS, BAGS, AND EVEN SWEATERS.

WELL, NOW YOU KNOW HOW TO CAST ON, CAST OFF AND JOIN IN A NEW BALL OF WOOL YOU CAN KNIT SCARVES IN ALL KINDS OF DIFFERENT WOOLS.

Tank tops

Now you've mastered garter stitch, try purl, and then you can make this tank top. The shaping is easy; two squares, one for the back and one for the front plus two straps which you can cross if you like. Made in double knitting, it is a simple, quick-to-knit summer top.

Materials

I'VE GOT SOMETHING TO DRINK AND THE SANDWICHES. SUSAN'S CARRYING THE DESSERT.

SHE'S BROUGHT HER KNITTING. SHE WANTS TO MAKE A TANK TOP.

YES, I'VE GOT A PAIR OF 4¹/2mm OR N°7 NEEDLES AND SEVEN 25gr BALLS PATONS TRIDENT DK.

21

Measurements

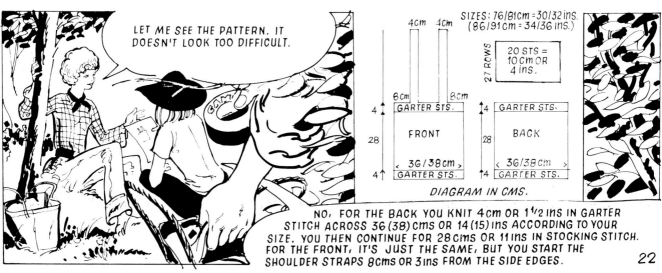

LET ME SEE THE PATTERN. IT DOESN'T LOOK TOO DIFFICULT.

SIZES: 76/81cm = 30/32 ins. (86/91cm = 34/36 ins.)

27 ROWS

20 STS = 10 CM OR 4 ins.

4cm   4cm

6cm   8cm

4   GARTER STS.

28   FRONT

36/38cm

4   GARTER STS.

4   GARTER STS.

28   BACK

36/38cm

4   GARTER STS.

DIAGRAM IN CMS.

NO, FOR THE BACK YOU KNIT 4cm OR 1¹/2 ins IN GARTER STITCH ACROSS 36 (38) CMS OR 14 (15) ins ACCORDING TO YOUR SIZE. YOU THEN CONTINUE FOR 28 cms OR 11 ins IN STOCKING STITCH. FOR THE FRONT, IT'S JUST THE SAME, BUT YOU START THE SHOULDER STRAPS 8 cms OR 3 ins FROM THE SIDE EDGES.

22

Stocking stitch

HOW DO YOU DO STOCKING STITCH?

YOU KNIT ONE ROW PLAIN, THEN ONE ROW PURL, AND REPEAT THESE TWO ROWS.

IT LOOKS LIKE THIS ON YOUR KNITTING. THIS IS THE RIGHT SIDE.

stocking stitch–right side showing 5 stitches per row.

stocking stitch–wrong side–showing there are 4 rows.

23

THE OTHER SIDE IS LIKE THIS. THIS IS THE WRONG SIDE.

Purl stitch

I CAN DO PLAIN... BUT... I CAN'T PURL.

IT'S SIMPLE – FOLLOW AS I SHOW YOU.

LOOK, THE YARN IS PULLED FORWARD.

YOU LOOP THE YARN AROUND THE NEEDLE BY PASSING IT OVER THE RIGHT-HAND NEEDLE.

24

PULL OUT THE NEEDLE AS YOU PULL THE YARN BACK. THE STITCH IS MADE AND YOU CAN DROP THE STITCH FROM THE LEFT-HAND NEEDLE.

The borders

I LIKE STOCKING STITCH, BUT WHAT WOULD HAPPEN IF YOU KNITTED IT ALL IN THAT STITCH?

THE KNITTING WOULD CURL UP, MAGGIE. UNLESS YOU PUT HEMS ALL ROUND THE EDGES AND THAT WOULDN'T BE VERY PRACTICAL FOR THE STRAPS. FOR THE LOWER EDGE OF YOUR KNITTING, USE STITCHES THAT DON'T CURL UP, LIKE GARTER STITCH, MOSS STITCH OR RIBBING.

The side edges and the back

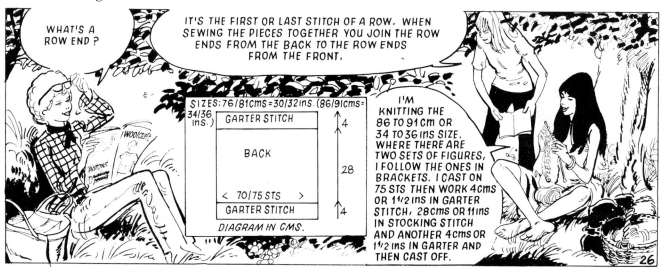

WHAT'S A ROW END?

IT'S THE FIRST OR LAST STITCH OF A ROW. WHEN SEWING THE PIECES TOGETHER YOU JOIN THE ROW ENDS FROM THE BACK TO THE ROW ENDS FROM THE FRONT.

SIZES: 76/81cms = 30/32 ins. (86/91cms = 34/36 ins.)

GARTER STITCH

BACK

4

28

< 70/75 STS >

GARTER STITCH

4

DIAGRAM IN CMS.

I'M KNITTING THE 86 TO 91CM OR 34 TO 36 INS SIZE. WHERE THERE ARE TWO SETS OF FIGURES, I FOLLOW THE ONES IN BRACKETS. I CAST ON 75 STS THEN WORK 4cms OR 1½ ins IN GARTER STITCH, 28cms OR 11ins IN STOCKING STITCH AND ANOTHER 4cms OR 1½ ins IN GARTER AND THEN CAST OFF.

The front

I KNITTED THE FRONT THE SAME AS THE BACK, BUT INSTEAD OF CASTING OFF I'VE GOT TO KNIT THE STRAPS NOW.

YOU CAST OFF 15 STITCHES (**1**) AND THEN WITH THE NEXT 8 STITCHES YOU KNIT 36 cms OR 14 ins IN GARTER STITCH TO FORM THE STRAP (**2**). CAST OFF THESE 8 STITCHES.

JOIN IN THE YARN TO FIRST OF REMAINING STITCHES AND CAST OFF THE NEXT 29 STITCHES (IF YOU WERE KNITTING THE SMALLER SIZE YOU WOULD CAST OFF 24 STITCHES). KNIT THE SECOND STRAP TO MATCH THE FIRST (**3**). THEN TO FINISH YOU CAST OFF REMAINING 15 STITCHES.

27

Invisible seams

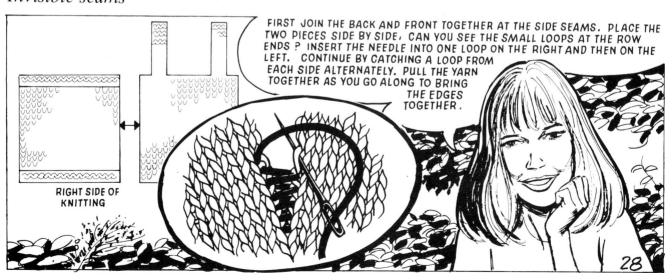

FIRST JOIN THE BACK AND FRONT TOGETHER AT THE SIDE SEAMS. PLACE THE TWO PIECES SIDE BY SIDE. CAN YOU SEE THE SMALL LOOPS AT THE ROW ENDS? INSERT THE NEEDLE INTO ONE LOOP ON THE RIGHT AND THEN ON THE LEFT. CONTINUE BY CATCHING A LOOP FROM EACH SIDE ALTERNATELY. PULL THE YARN TOGETHER AS YOU GO ALONG TO BRING THE EDGES TOGETHER.

RIGHT SIDE OF KNITTING

28

Oversewing

29

Tank top variations

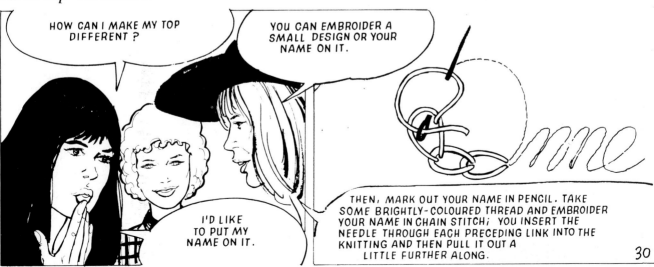

30

Stripy sweaters

Now you can knit plain and purl. Using these two stitches there are over 100 different stitch patterns you can knit. Here's one, called moss stitch. It's used for the main part of this oversweater, alternating with bands of garter stitch. Make it in soft, pure wool and wear it on its own in spring or over a blouse in winter.

Materials

THAT SWEATER IS GORGEOUS... DO YOU THINK I COULD MAKE IT?

woolcraft

IT'S NOT DIFFICULT. IT'S AN OVERSWEATER KNITTED IN MOSS STITCH AND GARTER STITCH.

YOU NEED SIX 50gm BALLS OF PATONS HUSKY IN NATURAL, TWO BALLS IN GREEN AND FIVE BALLS IN BLUE AND A PAIR OF LONG 6½mm OR Nº3 NEEDLES.

AND I'LL TAKE THIS OPPORTUNITY TO SHOW YOU SOME MORE STITCHES.

PATONS

Casting on – the thumb method

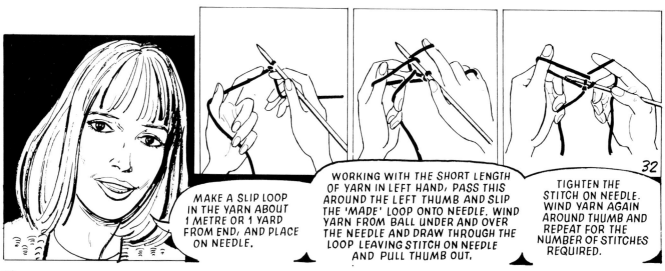

MAKE A SLIP LOOP IN THE YARN ABOUT 1 METRE OR 1 YARD FROM END, AND PLACE ON NEEDLE.

WORKING WITH THE SHORT LENGTH OF YARN IN LEFT HAND, PASS THIS AROUND THE LEFT THUMB AND SLIP THE 'MADE' LOOP ONTO NEEDLE. WIND YARN FROM BALL UNDER AND OVER THE NEEDLE AND DRAW THROUGH THE LOOP LEAVING STITCH ON NEEDLE AND PULL THUMB OUT.

TIGHTEN THE STITCH ON NEEDLE. WIND YARN AGAIN AROUND THUMB AND REPEAT FOR THE NUMBER OF STITCHES REQUIRED.

Moss stitch

IT SAYS, "MOSS STITCH * 1 STITCH PLAIN, 1 STITCH PURL*; REPEAT FROM* TO* TO END OF ROW." WHAT DO THE ASTERISKS MEAN?

THAT YOU HAVE TO REPEAT THE INSTRUCTIONS BETWEEN THE ASTERISKS FOR AS MANY TIMES AS NECESSARY TO FINISH THE ROW, OR AS OFTEN AS YOU ARE INSTRUCTED.

33

How to hold the yarn

DON'T FORGET, MAGGIE, IF YOU HAVE KNITTED A PLAIN STITCH AND YOU WANT TO DO A PURL STITCH, YOU HAVE TO BRING THE YARN FORWARD BETWEEN THE NEEDLES. YOU PUT IT BACK AGAIN AFTER THE PURL STITCH.

FOR MOSS STITCH, I REVERSE THE STITCHES ON THE NEXT ROW, KNITTING PLAIN THE PURL STITCHES, AND PURLING THE PLAIN STITCHES. THESE TWO ROWS ARE REPEATED FOR THE LENGTH REQUIRED.

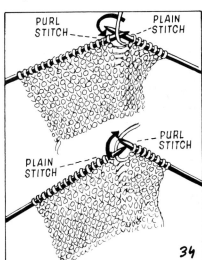

PURL STITCH

PLAIN STITCH

PLAIN STITCH

PURL STITCH

34

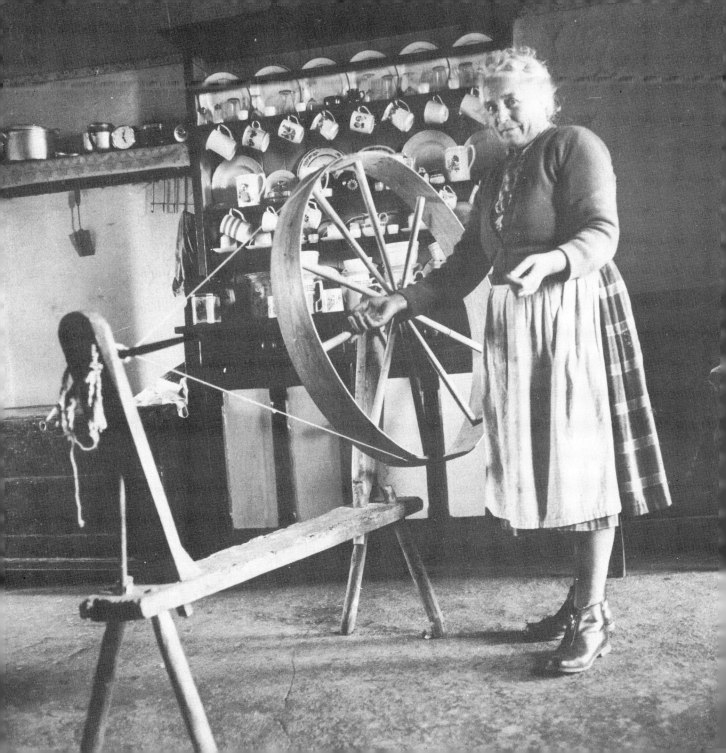

Knitting in stripes

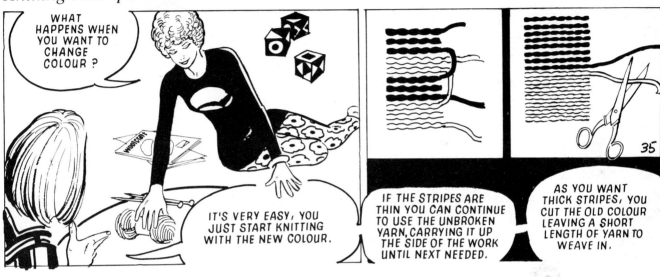

WHAT HAPPENS WHEN YOU WANT TO CHANGE COLOUR?

IT'S VERY EASY, YOU JUST START KNITTING WITH THE NEW COLOUR.

IF THE STRIPES ARE THIN YOU CAN CONTINUE TO USE THE UNBROKEN YARN, CARRYING IT UP THE SIDE OF THE WORK UNTIL NEXT NEEDED.

AS YOU WANT THICK STRIPES, YOU CUT THE OLD COLOUR LEAVING A SHORT LENGTH OF YARN TO WEAVE IN.

35

The front

I'M MAKING THE 81 TO 86 cm OR 32 TO 34 ins SIZE, SO I CAST ON 57 STITCHES AND KNIT 21 ROWS OF EACH COLOUR. I AM GOING TO USE MOSS STITCH FOR THE NATURAL WOOL AND GARTER STITCH FOR THE BLUE AND GREEN.

DO REMEMBER TO REVERSE THE STITCHES FOR THE MOSS STITCH, SO THAT IF THE NEXT STITCH ON THE LEFT-HAND NEEDLE IS A PLAIN STITCH YOU MUST PURL IT. AS YOU HAVE AN UNEVEN NUMBER OF STITCHES ON THE NEEDLE FOR THIS PATTERN, EVERY ROW WILL BEGIN AND END WITH A PLAIN STITCH.

SIZES: 81/86 cms = 32/34 ins.
(91/96 cms = 36/38 ins.)

44 (47) cms

MOSS STS	
GARTER STS	
MOSS STS	
GARTER STS	
MOSS STS	
22.5 (24)	
GARTER STS	
MOSS STS	
GARTER STS	
MOSS STS	
GARTER STS	
MOSS STS	

31 STS — 31 STS
31 STS — 31 STS
36 / 36 / 36
22 ROWS / 13 STS 10 cm or 4 ins
21 ROWS

44 (47) cms

DIAGRAM IN CMS

SIZES: 81/86 cms = 32/34 ins.
(91/96 cms = 36/38 ins.)

57 (61) STS

NATURAL	
BLUE	
NATURAL	
GREEN	
NATURAL	
27 (29) BLUE	
NATURAL	
GREEN	
NATURAL	
BLUE	
NATURAL	

38 STS — 38 STS
53 (54) STS — 53 (54) STS
38 STS — 38 STS
36 cm / 36 cm / 36 cm
13 STS = 10 cms or 4 ins
21 ROWS

57 (61) STS

DIAGRAM IN STITCHES

36

Casting on extra stitches

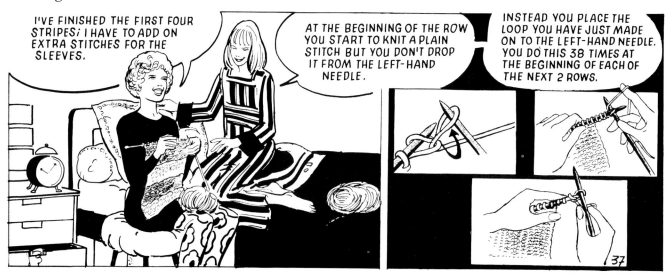

I'VE FINISHED THE FIRST FOUR STRIPES; I HAVE TO ADD ON EXTRA STITCHES FOR THE SLEEVES.

AT THE BEGINNING OF THE ROW YOU START TO KNIT A PLAIN STITCH BUT YOU DON'T DROP IT FROM THE LEFT-HAND NEEDLE.

INSTEAD YOU PLACE THE LOOP YOU HAVE JUST MADE ON TO THE LEFT-HAND NEEDLE. YOU DO THIS 38 TIMES AT THE BEGINNING OF EACH OF THE NEXT 2 ROWS.

Shaping the slash neckline

LOOK AT THE SLEEVES. I'VE DONE 21 ROWS IN NATURAL AND 20 ROWS IN BLUE.

THEN YOU'VE REACHED THE NECK. DON'T CHANGE COLOUR. KNIT THE FIRST 53(54) STS, CAST OFF THE CENTRE 27(29) STS AND THEN CONTINUE TO THE END OF THE ROW. ON THE NEXT ROW WHEN YOU REACH THE NECK OPENING YOU TURN AND CAST ON 27(29) STS, THEN TURN AND CONTINUE TO THE END OF THE ROW. THIS COMPLETES THE NECK OPENING.

38

The back

AFTER WORKING THE NECK OPENING YOU CONTINUE FOR 20 MORE ROWS IN BLUE, THEN 19 ROWS IN NATURAL AND CAST OFF 38 STS AT THE BEGINNING OF THE NEXT 2 ROWS TO COMPLETE THE SLEEVES.

THEN I HAVE THE SAME NUMBER OF STITCHES AS WHEN I STARTED.

SO YOU CONTINUE WITH ONE STRIPE GREEN, ONE NATURAL, ONE BLUE AND ONE NATURAL. THEN CAST OFF LOOSELY WITH NATURAL.

39

Completing the sweater and variations

YOU CATCH UP THE ENDS OF THE YARN AS YOU JOIN THE SEAMS. USE SMALL BACK STITCHES ONE STITCH IN FROM THE EDGE, AS ILLUSTRATED, BY THE DOTTED LINES ON THE DIAGRAM.

YOU CAN KNIT THIS SWEATER ALL IN GARTER STITCH OR ALL IN MOSS STITCH. YOU COULD ALSO KNIT THINNER STRIPES OR MAKE IT ALL IN ONE COLOUR. I'M GOING TO KNIT A MINI VERSION FOR MY LITTLE COUSIN'S TEDDY BEAR.

40

Woolly waistcoats

Knitted in a thick yarn and mohair, this waistcoat is both lightweight and hardwearing. To make it you'll have to learn to decrease for the shaping – but don't worry, it's not very difficult. And as this pattern is knitted all in one piece, it's very easy to make up. All you have to do is to join the shoulder seams.

Materials

Rice stitch

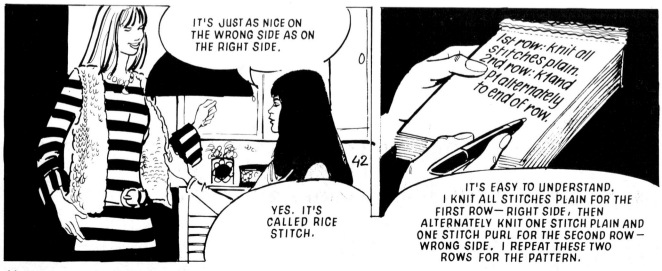

Slipping a stitch

THERE ARE THREE PLAIN STITCHES AT THE BEGINNING AND END OF EVERY ROW TO MARK THE FRONT EDGES.

IF YOU WANT A NEATER EDGE, YOU CAN SLIP THE FIRST STITCH ON EACH ROW. THAT IS, INSERT THE NEEDLE INTO THIS STITCH BUT SLIP IT OFF THE LEFT-HAND NEEDLE AND ON TO THE RIGHT-HAND NEEDLE WITHOUT KNITTING IT.

43

Shaping

I'M MAKING THIS WAISTCOAT FOR MUMMY. SHE NEEDS THE 91(96) CM OR 36(38) INS SIZE.

CAST ON 135 STITCHES AND KNIT 6 ROWS IN GARTER STITCH; CONTINUE IN RICE STITCH FOR THE CENTRE 129 STITCHES. FOR A SMALLER SIZE YOU ONLY NEED TO CAST ON 123 STS.

17(19) STS

35 CMS

WHEN YOUR KNITTING MEASURES 35 CMS OR 13½ INS ENDING WITH A RIGHT-SIDE ROW, YOU SHAPE THE ARMHOLES. WORK 3 STITCHES IN GARTER STITCH, 20(22) STS IN RICE STITCH, 17(19) STS IN GARTER STITCH, 43(47) STS IN RICE STITCH, 17(19) STS IN GARTER STITCH, 20(22) STS IN RICE STITCH, AND 3 STS IN GARTER STITCH. YOU REPEAT THIS ROW 4 TIMES. ON THE NEXT ROW – RIGHT-SIDE – CAST OF 11(13) STS IN THE CENTRE OF THE GARTER STITCH BANDS FOR THE ARMHOLES.

44

Shaping – back and front

NOW I KNIT THE BACKS AND FRONTS SEPARATELY?

YOU'RE REALLY KNITTING QUICKLY.

YES, FOR THE FRONTS YOU CONTINUE UNTIL YOU REACH 43CMS OR 17INS FROM CAST-ON EDGE, THEN FOR THE NECK SHAPING YOU DECREASE ONE STITCH ON EVERY RIGHT-SIDE ROW UNTIL 14 (15) STS REMAIN. WHEN YOUR KNITTING MEASURES 60CM OR 23½ INS YOU CAST OFF.

Simple decreasing

SIMPLE DECREASINGS

I'M DOING THE LEFT SIDE OF THE FRONT. I'VE GOT TO THE DECREASINGS.

KNIT UNTIL 5 STITCHES REMAIN THEN AS YOU WANT TO DECREASE WITH A RIGHT-HAND SLANT, KNIT THE NEXT 2 STITCHES TOGETHER BY INSERTING THE NEEDLE INTO THE SECOND STITCH AND THEN INTO THE FIRST STITCH, KNIT PLAIN THE LAST 3 STITCHES.

Slip decreasing

I'VE KNITTED THE BACK STRAIGHT AND CAST OFF. NOW DO I KNIT THE RIGHT SIDE TO CORRESPOND WITH THE LEFT?

YES. WHEN YOU GET TO THE SHAPING WITH THE RIGHT-SIDE OF WORK FACING YOU KNIT 3 STS IN GARTER STITCH FOR THE FRONT EDGE, THEN SLIP THE NEXT STITCH; KNIT THE NEXT STITCH WITH THE LEFT-HAND NEEDLE, PASS THE SLIPPED STITCH OVER THE KNITTED STITCH AND OFF THE NEEDLE.

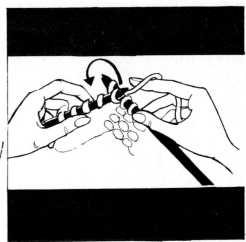

47

Completing the waistcoat and variations

YOU'VE FINISHED ALREADY?

I HAVE JUST GOT TO BACK STITCH THE SHOULDERS TOGETHER.

TO BRIGHTEN UP THIS WAISTCOAT YOU CAN USE SEVERAL SHADES OF KISMET TO GIVE A MULTI-COLOURED EFFECT. YOU CAN ALSO KNIT 3 PLAIN AND 3 PURL ON THE WRONG SIDE.

48

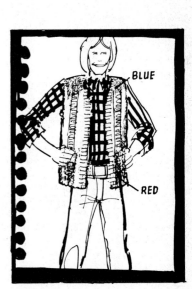

BLUE

RED

Stocking stitch sweaters

Made in machine-washable Capstan, this easy-knit sweater is both casual and comfortable. The shape is very simple – just four rectangles. If you're feeling ambitious, you can knit on the sleeves, otherwise make them separately and stitch them in position afterwards. You can also introduce a simple three-row lace pattern into the sleeves, by working two plain rows and knitting a row of 'holes' in between!

Materials

I LIKE THAT SWEATER, IS IT COMPLICATED TO MAKE?

NO, BUT IF YOU'RE A BEGINNER KNIT THE SLEEVES SEPARATELY AND DON'T BOTHER TO WORK THE CHAIN EDGE. YOU ARE MAKING THE 81 (86) cm OR 32 (34) INS SIZE SO YOU WILL NEED 10 50gr BALLS OF PATONS CAPSTAN AND A PAIR OF 4¹/2mm OR Nº 7 NEEDLES. FOR THE LARGER SIZE YOU WOULD NEED 11 BALLS OF CAPSTAN.

SIZES: 81/86cm = 32/34 INS (91/96cm=36/38ins)

Lace stitch band

THE LACE STITCH BAND IS KNITTED OVER 3 ROWS. ROW 1 AND 3: ON THE WRONG SIDE OF THE WORK YOU JUST KNIT ALL STITCHES PLAIN. ROW 2: K1, ✱ WIND YARN AROUND THE RIGHT-HAND NEEDLE TO MAKE A STITCH, THEN K2 TOGETHER; REPEAT FROM ✱ TO THE END OF THE ROW.

SO I KNIT 2 STITCHES TOGETHER AS FOR DECREASING?

YES, TO MAKE THE STITCH YOU WIND THE YARN AROUND THE NEEDLE FROM THE BACK TO THE FRONT AND OVER THE NEEDLE TO THE BACK AGAIN.

50

Chain edge

I CAST ON 83 STS THEN KNIT 3 cms OR 1¼ ins IN STOCKING STITCH. THEN I PURL 1 ROW ON THE RIGHT SIDE OF WORK TO MARK THE HEM. I CONTINUE IN STOCKING STITCH BEGINNING WITH ANOTHER PURL ROW UNTIL WORK MEASURES 55 cm OR 21½ ins FROM CAST-ON EDGE. I THEN WORK ANOTHER HEM ROW, 7 ROWS MORE IN STOCKING STITCH AND CAST OFF.

IF YOU WANT TO KNIT ON THE SLEEVES, WHEN YOUR WORK MEASURES 37 cm OR 14½ ins FROM BEGINNING YOU SLIP THE FIRST STITCH ON ALL ROWS, THIS WILL GIVE YOU A CHAIN EDGE.

51

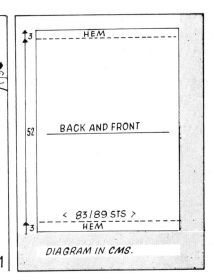

HEM
3
52
BACK AND FRONT
< 83/89 STS >
3
HEM

DIAGRAM IN CMS.

Making a hem

I'VE FINISHED THE BACK AND FRONT.

ARE THEY BOTH 58 cms OR 23 ins AND HAVE YOU WORKED THE TOP HEM? FINE. ALL YOU HAVE TO DO NOW IS FOLD THE KNITTING ALONG THE TOP HEM LINE AND CAST-OFF STITCHES TO THE WRONG SIDE OF THE KNITTING.

52

Picking up stitches

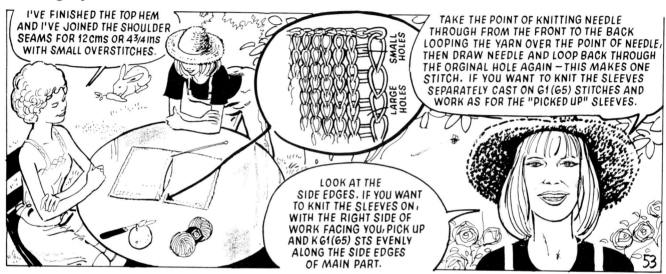

The sleeves

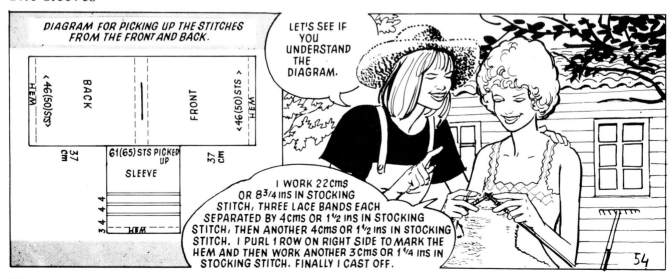

Making the drawstring

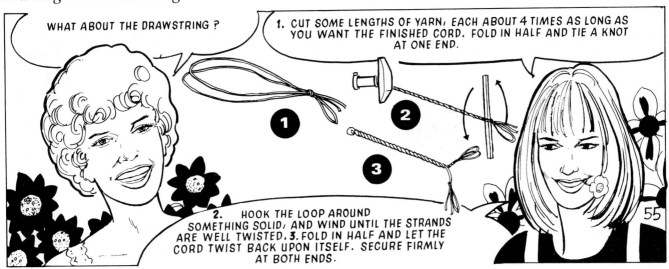

WHAT ABOUT THE DRAWSTRING ?

1. CUT SOME LENGTHS OF YARN, EACH ABOUT 4 TIMES AS LONG AS YOU WANT THE FINISHED CORD. FOLD IN HALF AND TIE A KNOT AT ONE END.

2. HOOK THE LOOP AROUND SOMETHING SOLID, AND WIND UNTIL THE STRANDS ARE WELL TWISTED. 3. FOLD IN HALF AND LET THE CORD TWIST BACK UPON ITSELF. SECURE FIRMLY AT BOTH ENDS.

55

Completing the sweater

I'VE JOINED THE SIDE AND SLEEVE SEAMS AND CAUGHT THE HEMS IN POSITION, REMEMBERING TO LEAVE A SMALL OPENING IN THE LOWER HEM TO THREAD THE DRAWSTRING THROUGH.

THAT'S MARVELLOUS. NOW THREAD THE DRAWSTRING THROUGH THE HEM AND DRAW UP SLIGHTLY.

56

Chunky cable sweaters

Don't think that cable patterns are only for experienced knitters. Make this sweater and see just how simple they can be. It's just a matter of switching one set of stitches for another at regular intervals. There are also step-by-step instructions showing you how to knit a neckband, using four double-pointed needles.

Materials

I'D LIKE A PAIR OF 6½mm OR N° 3 NEEDLES AND TWELVE 50gr BALLS OF PATONS HUSKY TO MAKE THIS SWEATER. CAN YOU PLEASE EXPLAIN HOW I WORK THE CABLES?

INSTEAD OF KNITTING THE STITCHES IN THE USUAL ORDER AS THEY ARE ON THE LEFT-HAND NEEDLE, YOU KNIT STITCHES 4, 5 AND 6 AND THEN STITCHES 1, 2 AND 3. YOU WILL NEED A CABLE NEEDLE OR A SHORT DOUBLE-POINTED NEEDLE ON WHICH TO SLIP THE FIRST THREE STITCHES WHILE YOU ARE KNITTING THE OTHER THREE.

Cable pattern

MAY I SEE THAT CABLE?

THE CABLE PANEL IS KNITTED OVER 14 STITCHES. FOUR STITCHES ON EITHER SIDE OF THE CABLE ARE WORKED IN GARTER STITCH FOR THE BACKGROUND. THE CENTRE 6 STITCHES FOR THE CABLE ITSELF ARE IN STOCKING STITCH. YOU KNIT 4 ROWS STRAIGHT THEN WORK THE CABLE ON THE 5th ROW AND THEN ON EVERY FOLLOWING 8th ROW. WITH THE RIGHT SIDE OF WORK FACING YOU SLIP THE FIRST THREE CABLE STITCHES ON TO ANOTHER NEEDLE AND LEAVE AT THE BACK OF THE WORK, KNIT THE NEXT 3 STITCHES, THEN KNIT THE 3 STITCHES FROM SPARE NEEDLE.

Beaded edge

The sleeves

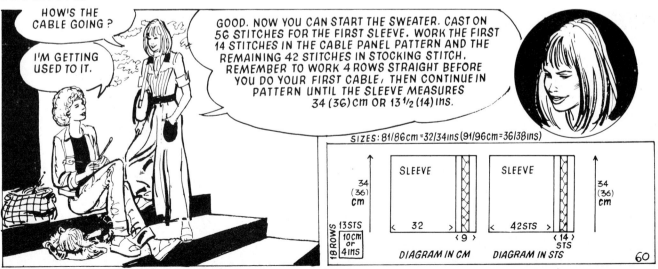

The back

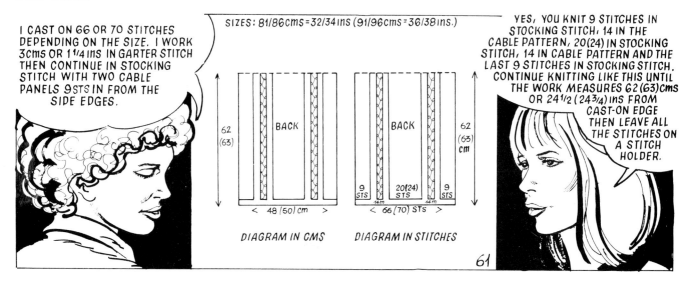

I CAST ON 66 OR 70 STITCHES DEPENDING ON THE SIZE. I WORK 3cms OR 1¼ ins IN GARTER STITCH THEN CONTINUE IN STOCKING STITCH WITH TWO CABLE PANELS 9STS IN FROM THE SIDE EDGES.

SIZES: 81/86cms = 32/34 ins (91/96cms = 36/38ins.)

YES, YOU KNIT 9 STITCHES IN STOCKING STITCH, 14 IN THE CABLE PATTERN, 20(24) IN STOCKING STITCH, 14 IN CABLE PATTERN AND THE LAST 9 STITCHES IN STOCKING STITCH. CONTINUE KNITTING LIKE THIS UNTIL THE WORK MEASURES 62(63)cms OR 24½ (24¾) ins FROM CAST-ON EDGE THEN LEAVE ALL THE STITCHES ON A STITCH HOLDER.

62 (63) cm

BACK

48 (50) cm

DIAGRAM IN CMS

62 (63) cm

BACK

9 STS   20(24) STS   9 STS
14m   44m

66 (70) STS

DIAGRAM IN STITCHES

61

The front

IS THE FRONT THE SAME AS THE BACK?

YOU START IN THE SAME WAY, BUT WHEN THE WORK MEASURES 55(56)cms OR 21¾(22) ins YOU SHAPE THE NECK. ON THE NEXT ROW, WHEN YOU HAVE KNITTED THE CENTRE 14 STS YOU SLIP THEM ON TO A STITCH HOLDER UNTIL REQUIRED FOR THE NECKBAND AND CONTINUE EACH SHOULDER SEPARATELY.

7 cm

17(18)   14   17(18)

55 (56)

FRONT

48 (50) cm

DIAGRAM IN CMS

13 STS
10 cm or 4 ins
18 ROWS

FOR EACH SHOULDER YOU DECREASE ONE STITCH AT THE NECK EDGE ON THE NEXT 2 RIGHT-SIDE ROWS. CONTINUE STRAIGHT ON REMAINING 24(26) STITCHES UNTIL THE WORK MEASURES THE SAME AS THE BACK. LEAVE STITCHES ON SPARE NEEDLES.

24(26)   18   24(26)

14

7 cm

FRONT

55 (56) cm

9   20(24)   9
14   14

66 (70)

DIAGRAM IN STITCHES

62

Knitting the shoulder seams together

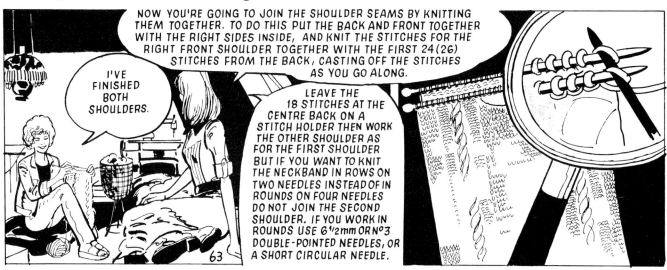

NOW YOU'RE GOING TO JOIN THE SHOULDER SEAMS BY KNITTING THEM TOGETHER. TO DO THIS PUT THE BACK AND FRONT TOGETHER WITH THE RIGHT SIDES INSIDE, AND KNIT THE STITCHES FOR THE RIGHT FRONT SHOULDER TOGETHER WITH THE FIRST 24(26) STITCHES FROM THE BACK, CASTING OFF THE STITCHES AS YOU GO ALONG.

I'VE FINISHED BOTH SHOULDERS.

LEAVE THE 18 STITCHES AT THE CENTRE BACK ON A STITCH HOLDER THEN WORK THE OTHER SHOULDER AS FOR THE FIRST SHOULDER BUT IF YOU WANT TO KNIT THE NECKBAND IN ROWS ON TWO NEEDLES INSTEAD OF IN ROUNDS ON FOUR NEEDLES DO NOT JOIN THE SECOND SHOULDER. IF YOU WORK IN ROUNDS USE 6½mm OR Nº3 DOUBLE-POINTED NEEDLES, OR A SHORT CIRCULAR NEEDLE.

63

The neckband

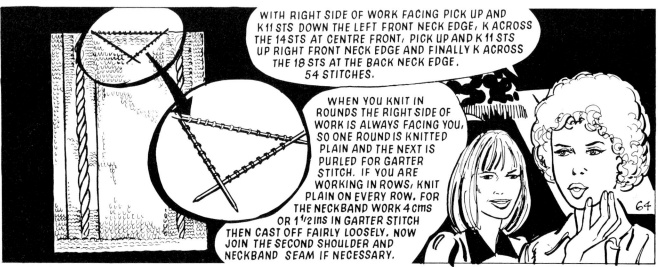

WITH RIGHT SIDE OF WORK FACING PICK UP AND K 11 STS DOWN THE LEFT FRONT NECK EDGE, K ACROSS THE 14 STS AT CENTRE FRONT, PICK UP AND K 11 STS UP RIGHT FRONT NECK EDGE AND FINALLY K ACROSS THE 18 STS AT THE BACK NECK EDGE. 54 STITCHES.

WHEN YOU KNIT IN ROUNDS THE RIGHT SIDE OF WORK IS ALWAYS FACING YOU, SO ONE ROUND IS KNITTED PLAIN AND THE NEXT IS PURLED FOR GARTER STITCH. IF YOU ARE WORKING IN ROWS, KNIT PLAIN ON EVERY ROW. FOR THE NECKBAND WORK 4 CMS OR 1½ INS IN GARTER STITCH THEN CAST OFF FAIRLY LOOSELY. NOW JOIN THE SECOND SHOULDER AND NECKBAND SEAM IF NECESSARY.

64

Knitting in rounds

WHEN KNITTING IN ROUNDS YOU NEED 4 NEEDLES WITHOUT KNOBS, DIVIDE THE STITCHES EQUALLY ON TO THREE NEEDLES THEN KNIT WITH THE FOURTH...

... ALWAYS GOING IN THE SAME DIRECTION AND MAKING SURE THAT THE YARN IS HELD FIRMLY WHEN PASSING FROM ONE NEEDLE TO ANOTHER. IF YOU PREFER YOU CAN USE A SHORT CIRCULAR NEEDLE INSTEAD.

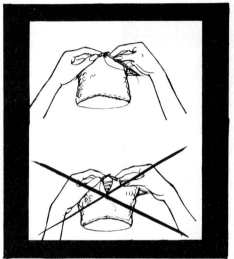

Husky polo necks

How you ever looked at a Fair-Isle sweater and thought you would like
to knit one? Well here's your chance to learn. Designed with raglan
sleeves, two very simple Fair-Isle patterns are introduced into this
quick-to-knit sweater. If you're not very patient, but still want to make a
polo neck sweater, just follow the instructions and replace the Fair-Isle
with simple stripes.

Materials

HAVE YOU GOT EVERTHING YOU NEED FOR THE POLO NECK SWEATER?

YES, 11 (12) 50gr BALLS OF PATONS HUSKY IN NATURAL AND ONE BALL EACH IN BLUE AND NAVY. I ALSO HAVE A PAIR OF 6½mm OR Nº3 NEEDLES. IT'S A LOVELY SWEATER — I BET JOHN WILL WANT TO BORROW IT!

SIZES: 81/86cm = 32/34ins
(91/96cm = 36/38ins)

62cm

28 (35)

38 (42)

38 (42)

13 STS
10 cm
4 ins

18 ROWS

47 (51)

40 cm

62 cm

4

67

DIAGRAM IN STITCHES

Two and two ribbing

I'VE NEVER DONE ANY RIBBING.

IT'S A STITCH THAT YOU USE WHEN YOU WANT TO GIVE ELASTICITY TO YOUR KNITTING, FOR NECKS OR WRISTS...

2/2 RIBBING – ROW 1: ✱ K2, P2, REPEAT FROM ✱ TO END. ON THE FOLLOWING ROWS KNIT THE STITCHES AS THEY OCCUR.

THAT MEANS YOU KNIT PLAIN ALL PLAIN STITCHES AND PURL ALL PURL STITCHES.

68

The sleeves

DO YOU BEGIN WITH THE SLEEVES?

YES, I'VE MARKED ALL THE MEASUREMENTS ON THE DIAGRAM.

CAST ON 36(40) STITCHES AND WORK 4cms OR 1½ ins IN K2, P2 RIB. WORK 2 ROWS IN STOCKING STITCH THEN CONTINUING IN STOCKING STITCH INCREASE 1 STITCH AT BOTH ENDS OF NEXT ROW AND EVERY FOLLOWING 10th ROW UNTIL THERE ARE 50(54) STITCHES. TO INCREASE YOU KNIT INTO THE FRONT AND BACK OF THE SAME STITCH, THUS MAKING TWO STITCHES OUT OF ONE STITCH.

19(21) cm
50(54)
SLEEVE
38 cm
PATTERN 1
4cm
2/2 RIB
36(40)
X = INCREASE
DIAGRAM IN STITCHES

69

Fair-Isle pattern

YOU'RE GETTING AMBITIOUS. WHY NOT KNIT A FAIR-ISLE PATTERN INTO THE SLEEVES?

YOU SHOULD START THE PATTERN ON THE 5th STOCKING STITCH ROW. IT'S ONLY A SMALL PATTERN, THE MOTIFS ARE MADE UP OF SIMPLE STRIPES AND ROWS WHERE YOU KNIT 2 STITCHES IN ONE COLOUR AND 2 STITCHES IN ANOTHER.

1ST MOTIF OVER 7 ROWS:
ROWS 1, 2, 6, 7 – ALL BLUE.
ROWS 3, 4, 5 – WORK 2 STS BLUE AND 2 STS NATURAL, ALTERNATELY.

70

Fair-Isle – watch the colours

2nd MOTIF OVER 8 ROWS:
ROWS 1, 2, 6, 7 – ALL NAVY.
ROWS 3, 4, 5, 8 – WORK 2 STITCHES NAVY, AND 2 NATURAL, ALTERNATELY.

IS THAT RIGHT?

YOU'VE CROSSED THE THREADS AS YOU SHOULD ON THE WRONG SIDE, BUT BE CAREFUL, DON'T PULL THE YARN TOO TIGHTLY WHEN YOU CHANGE COLOUR. LOOK BEHIND AND MAKE SURE THE STITCHES ARE NOT PULLING. IF YOU FIND THIS DIFFICULT, TRY KNITTING THE FAIR-ISLE PATTERNING ON NEEDLES A SIZE LARGER.

Sleeve decreasings

I'VE WORKED THE FIRST MOTIF AND ALL THE INCREASES AND THEN KNITTED A FEW ROWS STRAIGHT, MY KNITTING NOW MEASURES 42cms OR 16½ ins AS IN THE DIAGRAM. I'VE FINISHED WITH A PURL ROW.

CAST OFF 4 STITCHES AT THE BEGINNING OF EACH OF THE NEXT 2 ROWS. 3rd ROW: K1, K2 TOGETHER, K UNTIL 3 STITCHES REMAIN, SLIP 1, K1, PASS THE SLIPPED STITCH OVER, THEN K THE LAST STITCH. 4th ROW: ALL P. REPEAT THE LAST 2 ROWS 15 (17) TIMES. LEAVE REMAINING 10 STITCHES ON A STITCH HOLDER.

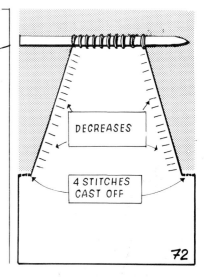

DECREASES

4 STITCHES CAST OFF

72

The back and front

CAST ON 60 (64) STITCHES AND WORK 6 ROWS IN K2, P2 RIB. WORK 4 ROWS IN STOCKING STITCH INCREASING 1 STITCH AT BOTH ENDS OF THE FIRST ROW. 62(66) STS. WORK THE 7 ROWS OF FIRST PATTERN, 3 ROWS IN STOCKING STITCH WITH NATURAL AND THEN THE EIGHT ROWS OF SECOND PATTERN. CONTINUE STRAIGHT WITH NATURAL UNTIL WORK MEASURES 44CMS OR 17½ INS ENDING WITH A PURL ROW. NOW SHAPE THE THE TOP AS FOR THE SLEEVES. 22 STS. LEAVE STITCHES ON A STITCH HOLDER.

Diagram labels: < 22 >; 19(21) cm; 4; 4; 40 cm; BACK AND FRONT; PATTERN 1; PATTERN 2; 4 cm; 2/2 RIB; < 60 (64) >; DIAGRAM IN STITCHES

The neckband

I'VE FINISHED THE FOUR PIECES.

TAKE THE FRONT STITCHES. CAST OFF THE FIRST STITCH, KNIT UNTIL 1 STITCH REMAINS, THEN CAST OFF THIS STITCH, PICK UP ONE SLEEVE AND CAST OFF THE FIRST STITCH, KNIT UNTIL 1 STITCH REMAINS THEN CAST OFF THIS STITCH, CONTINUE LIKE THIS FOR THE BACK AND THE SECOND SLEEVE. 56 STS NOW ON THE NEEDLE. WORK 20CM OR 8 INS. IN K2, P2 RIB THEN CAST OFF LOOSELY.

Completion and invisible seams

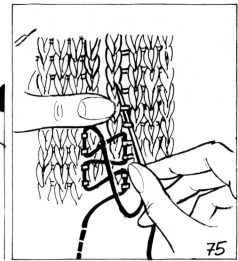

Fair-Isle variations

Jaunty jackets

You've already knitted three of four patterns, so now you're ready to
attempt something a little more complicated. Why not make this jacket,
complete with slit pockets and ribbed collar? Made in a chunky tweed
yarn it will be an asset to any wardrobe.

Materials

YOUR JACKET LOOKS NICE AND WARM. WOULD YOU MIND IF I MADE ONE LIKE IT?

OF COURSE NOT. ALL YOU NEED IS 11(12) 50gr BALLS OF PATONS HUSKY IN TWEED AND 4 BALLS IN A PLAIN COLOUR, 6 BUTTONS AND A PAIR EACH OF 6mm OR No4 NEEDLES AND 6½mm OR No3 NEEDLES. LOOK CAREFULLY AT THE DIAGRAMS. YOU SHOULD BE ABLE TO WORK OUT MOST OF THE INSTRUCTIONS.

SIZES: 81/86cm=32/34ins (91/96cm=36/38ins.)

15 (16) STS   20(22) STS

52(54)STS

42 cms

8 cms

13 STS
18 ROWS
10cm or 4ins

77

The back

7(8) 8(8)STS   (8)8(8)7STS

7STS

50(54)STS

BACK

7STS

20 (21) cm

40 cm

8 cm

64(68)STS
SIZES: 81/86cm=32/34ins.
(91/96cm=36/38ins)

I HAVE TO CAST ON 64(68) STITCHES WITH THE 6mm NEEDLES AND PLAIN YARN AND WORK 8cms OR 3ins IN K2, P2 RIB. THEN I CHANGE TO THE LARGER NEEDLES AND THE TWEED. I WORK 40cms OR 16ins IN STOCKING STITCH AND THEN CAST OFF 7 STITCHES AT THE BEGINNING OF EACH OF THE NEXT 2 ROWS FOR THE ARMHOLES.

AFTER THE ARMHOLE SHAPING YOU CONTINUE STRAIGHT FOR 20 (21) CMS OR 8 (8¼) INS.

78

Sloping the shoulders

YOU SLOPE THE SHOULDERS BY CASTING OFF 7(8) STITCHES AT THE BEGINNING OF EACH OF THE NEXT 2 ROWS AND 8(8) STITCHES AT THE BEGINNING OF THE FOLLOWING 2 ROWS.

I THEN LEAVE THE REMAINING 20(22) STITCHES ON A STITCH HOLDER UNTIL REQUIRED FOR THE COLLAR.

STITCHES ON HOLDER

//////// = STITCHES CAST OFF ON FIRST SIZE.

79

Slit pockets

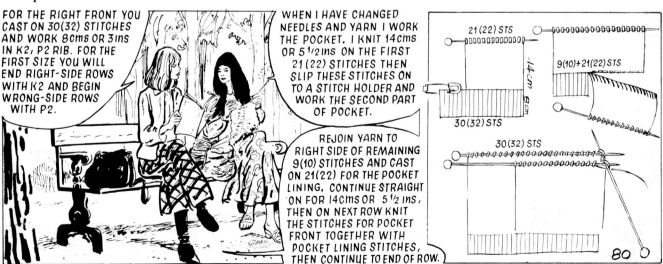

FOR THE RIGHT FRONT YOU CAST ON 30(32) STITCHES AND WORK 8cms OR 3ins IN K2, P2 RIB. FOR THE FIRST SIZE YOU WILL END RIGHT-SIDE ROWS WITH K2 AND BEGIN WRONG-SIDE ROWS WITH P2.

WHEN I HAVE CHANGED NEEDLES AND YARN I WORK THE POCKET. I KNIT 14cms OR 5½ins ON THE FIRST 21(22) STITCHES THEN SLIP THESE STITCHES ON TO A STITCH HOLDER AND WORK THE SECOND PART OF POCKET.

REJOIN YARN TO RIGHT SIDE OF REMAINING 9(10) STITCHES AND CAST ON 21(22) FOR THE POCKET LINING. CONTINUE STRAIGHT ON FOR 14cms OR 5½ ins, THEN ON NEXT ROW KNIT THE STITCHES FOR POCKET FRONT TOGETHER WITH POCKET LINING STITCHES, THEN CONTINUE TO END OF ROW.

21(22) STS

9(10)+21(22) STS

14cm

8cm

30(32) STS

30(32) STS

80

The fronts

DIAGRAM IN STITCHES

7(8) 8(8) STS

1 2 3(4)

7 STS | 23(25) STS

76 STS

62 cms.

18 STS
44 cm

9(10) | 21(22)

30 (32) STS

CONTINUE AS FOR THE BACK UNTIL WORK MEASURES 62cms OR 24½ ins ENDING AT CENTRE FRONT NECK EDGE. REMEMBER TO CAST OFF 7 STITCHES FOR THE ARMHOLE WHEN YOUR WORK MEASURES 48cms OR 19ins.

YES, THEN DECREASE 1 STITCH AT NECK EDGE ON NEXT ROW AND FOLLOWING 2 ALTERNATE ROWS WHEN 15(16) STITCHES WILL REMAIN. TO SLOPE THE SHOULDERS YOU CAST OFF 7(8) STITCHES, WORK 1 ROW STRAIGHT THEN CAST OFF REMAINING 8(8) STITCHES.

I CAST OFF 3(4) STITCHES AT NECK EDGE ON NEXT ROW AND 2 STITCHES ON FOLLOWING ALTERNATE ROW.

I THEN WORK THE LEFT FRONT IN THE SAME WAY BUT REVERSE ALL THE SHAPING.

81

Increasing in the middle of a row

YOU CAN KNIT THE SLEEVES NOW. CAST ON 36 STITCHES AND WORK 8cms OR 3ins IN K2, P2 RIB, THEN CONTINUE IN STOCKING STITCH WITH TWEED USING THE LARGER NEEDLES. YOU INCREASE ON THE FIRST ROW — K3 (1), *INC, K2 ; REPEAT FROM * ENDING LAST REPEAT K3(1). TO INCREASE ONE STITCH YOU INSERT THE NEEDLE INTO THE STITCH ON THE ROW BELOW AND KNIT IT — THIS MAKES AN EXTRA STITCH.

42 cm

52 (54) STS

8 cm

36 STS

I'VE GOT IT. I PUT THE NEEDLE IN UNDER EVERY SECOND STITCH.

82

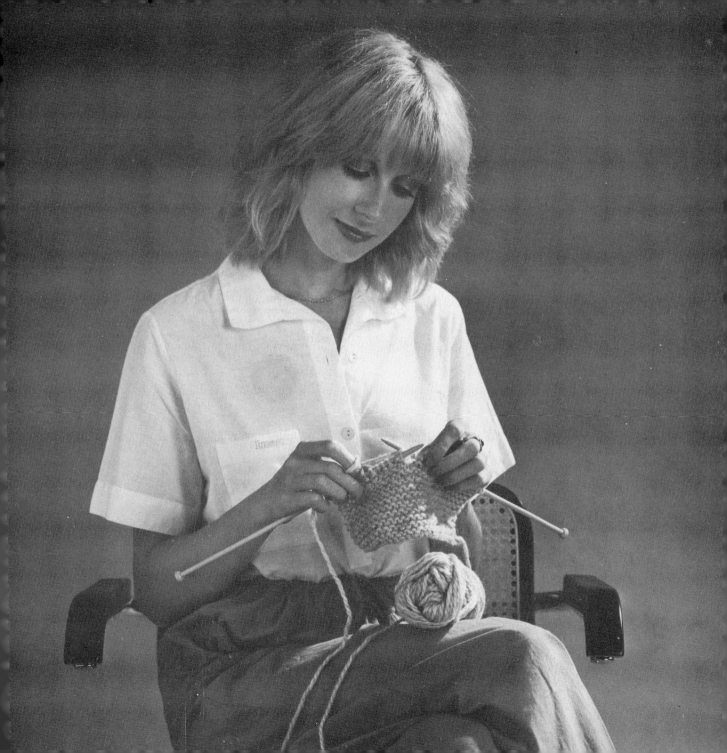

The sleeves

I'VE INCREASED AT THE WRISTS. I'VE GOT 52(54) STITCHES.

VERY GOOD. WORK 1 MORE ROW WITH TWEED THEN 2 ROWS WITH PLAIN, 2 WITH TWEED, 2 WITH PLAIN, 2 WITH TWEED, AND 2 WITH PLAIN. NOW CONTINUE WITH TWEED UNTIL WORK MEASURES 50 cms OR 20 ins. CAST OFF.

I'VE JOINED THE SHOULDER SEAMS, SET IN THE SLEEVES AND JOINED THE SLEEVE AND SIDE SEAMS.

YOU ONLY HAVE THE BORDERS LEFT. KNIT THEM WITH THE SMALLER NEEDLES SO THAT THEY ARE FIRM.

83

Front borders

FOR THE LEFT BORDER I PICK UP 76 STITCHES ?

THAT'S RIGHT, THEN YOU WORK 5 ROWS IN K2, P2 RIB. CAST OFF PLAINWISE. THE RIGHT BORDER IS THE SAME BUT ON THE 3rd ROW WORK SIX BUTTONHOLES AT EQUAL INTERVALS ALONG THE ROW.

76 STITCHES

84

The buttonholes

TO MAKE THE BUTTONHOLES, YOU CAST OFF 3 STITCHES AND CAST THEM ON AGAIN ON THE NEXT ROW. OR YOU CAN MAKE A LARGE HOLE BY KNITTING 2 STITCHES TOGETHER, WINDING THE YARN TWICE AROUND THE NEEDLE, AND KNITTING THE NEXT 2 STITCHES TOGETHER. ON THE NEXT ROW YOU KNIT INTO THE FRONT OF THE FIRST LOOP AND INTO THE BACK OF THE SECOND LOOP. WORK ROUND THE EDGE OF THE BUTTONHOLES IN BUTTONHOLE STITCH.

Borders for neck and pockets

SO I PICK UP 18 STITCHES ON EACH POCKET AND WORK 5 ROWS IN K2, P2 RIB ?

YES. NOW YOU ARE READY TO KNIT THE COLLAR. WITH THE WRONG SIDE OF WORK FACING AND USING THE FINER NEEDLES, PICK UP AND KNIT 62 STITCHES AROUND NECK EDGE INCLUDING THE STITCHES ON STITCH HOLDER. WORK 10 CMS OR 4 INS IN K2, P2 RIB THEN CHANGE TO THE THICKER NEEDLES AND RIB ANOTHER 10 CMS. CAST OFF IN RIB. NOW SEW ON THE BUTTONS AND CATCH DOWN THE POCKET BACKS AND THE JACKET IS FINISHED !

Pick up hints and dropped stitches

Disaster! It was all going fine until you dropped a couple of stitches, put your knitting down and forgot which way was up, twisted a few stitches, or – oh dear! – putting in the button holes would have helped! Never mind. Help is at hand – in this chapter. If you've made a mistake, or skipped a bit of the book, this is where to find the answers to your knitting problems.

Which way am I knitting?

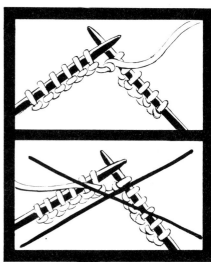

Casting off too tightly

IT'S BECAUSE YOU PULLED THE STITCHES TOO TIGHTLY. TRY CASTING OFF WITH A LARGER NEEDLE THAN YOU USED FOR THE MAIN PART OF THE KNITTING. IF NECESSARY YOU CAN DO THE SAME FOR CASTING ON.

Picking up a dropped stitch (plain)

HELP! I'VE DROPPED A STITCH AND IT'S RUN DOWN SEVERAL ROWS.

YOU'RE KNITTING STOCKING STITCH, SO TAKE A CROCHET HOOK, PICK UP THE STITCH ON THE RIGHT SIDE OF THE WORK IN FRONT OF THE BOTTOM LOOSE THREAD. PULL THIS THREAD THROUGH THE STITCH FROM BACK TO FRONT. CONTINUE IN THIS WAY UNTIL YOU ARE BACK TO THE STITCHES ON THE NEEDLE.

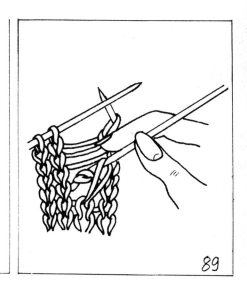

89

Picking up a dropped stitch (purl)

WHEN YOU ARE PICKING UP DROPPED PURL STITCHES SHOULD YOU HAVE THE OTHER SIDE OF THE WORK FACING YOU AND PICK THEM UP AS FOR PLAIN STITCHES?

YES. BUT IF YOU ARE KNITTING GARTER STITCH THIS DOESN'T WORK. YOU SHOULD PICK UP THE PURL STITCH BY INSERTING YOUR CROCHET HOOK INTO THE STITCH BEHIND THE LOOSE THREAD. PASS THIS THREAD THROUGH THE STITCH FROM FRONT TO BACK.

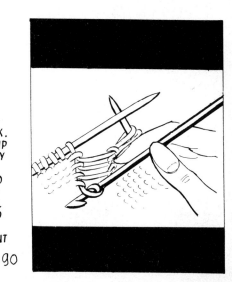

90

Untwisting stitches

WHEN I PICKED UP SOME DROPPED STITCHES I THINK I TWISTED THEM AROUND THE NEEDLE.

YOU'RE RIGHT. THESE STITCHES ARE TWISTED. TO UNTWIST THEM YOU INSERT YOUR NEEDLE INTO THE PART OF THE STITCH WHICH IS BEHIND THE LEFT-HAND NEEDLE INSTEAD OF IN FRONT OF IT. YOU CAN DELIBERATELY TWIST STITCHES IF YOU WANT TO KNIT CONTINENTAL STOCKING STITCH.

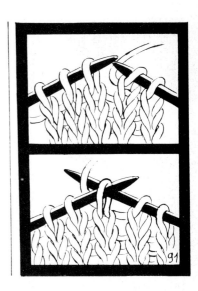

Undoing stitches and rows

I GOT CARRIED AWAY AND KNITTED 3 CMS TOO MUCH.

TAKE OUT THE NEEDLE AND PULL THE YARN GENTLY TO UNDO THE EXTRA ROWS, THEN PUT YOUR STITCHES BACK ON TO A THINNER NEEDLES — THIS MAKES IT EASIER TO PICK THEM UP AGAIN.

WHEN THERE ARE ONLY A FEW WRONG STITCHES, INSERT THE POINT OF THE RIGHT-HAND NEEDLE UNDER THE STITCH TO BE UNDONE BEFORE PULLING THE YARN OUT.

Sewing on neck edgings and borders

THIS SEWING IS DONE ON THE RIGHT SIDE OF THE WORK.

I DON'T LIKE PICKING UP STITCHES OR KNITTING IN ROUNDS.

YOU CAN KNIT THE NECK EDGE SEPARATELY AND SEW IT ON, WORKING THROUGH ONE STITCH IN THE EDGING AND ONE STITCH IN THE MAIN PART ALTERNATELY.

stitchcraft including needlewoman

93

Knitting two pieces alike

HOW DO I KNIT THESE TWO SLEEVES THE SAME WITHOUT COUNTING THE ROWS TO CHECK THAT THE INCREASES ARE IN THE RIGHT PLACE.

CAST ON THE STITCHES FOR BOTH SLEEVES ON TO THE SAME NEEDLE USING SEPARATE BALLS OF YARN. IF YOU KNIT ONE ROW FROM ONE SLEEVE AND THEN ONE ROW FROM THE OTHER YOU CAN'T GO WRONG.

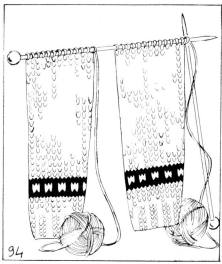

94

Adding a buttonhole

OH NO! I'VE FINISHED THE BORDERS AND I COMPLETELY FORGOT TO MAKE THE BUTTONHOLES!

IT'S ALRIGHT — YOU DON'T HAVE TO UNDO IT. RUN A ROW OF SMALL TIGHT RUNNING STITCHES AROUND THE SPOT WHERE THE BUTTONHOLE SHOULD BE.

95

THEN ALL YOU HAVE TO DO IS TO SLIT THE KNITTING INSIDE THE LINE OF RUNNING STITCHES AND VERY CAREFULLY CATCH UP THE STITCHES WITH BUTTONHOLE STITCH.

Adding at patch pocket

I FIND KNITTING POCKETS VERY BORING.

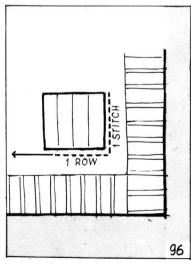

KNIT THE GARMENT WITHOUT POCKETS, THEN YOU CAN MAKE SEPARATE POCKETS AND SEW THEM ON. DO MAKE SURE THAT YOU SEW THE CAST-ON EDGE OF THE POCKET LEVEL WITH A ROW OF HORIZONTAL STITCHES AND THAT THE ROW ENDS OF POCKETS ARE IN A STRAIGHT LINE WITH THE VERTICAL STITCHES.

1 STITCH

1 ROW

96

Glossary and abbreviations

ADDING (a stitch)
Thus increasing (see INCREASING) This term is used especially when several stitches are added at once.

ASTERISKS *...*
Star-shaped sign used to section off any part of a pattern which must be repeated.

CAST OFF (a stitch)
Knit two stitches and pass the first one over the second and off the needle – thus decreasing one stitch.

CASTING ON
The name given to the stitches made at the beginning of a piece of knitting. Casting on is not counted as a row.

CATCHING UP A STITCH
Picking up a dropped stitch using a crochet hook.

DECREASING
Stitch taken out during knitting. There are many different methods of decreasing.

DROPPED STITCHES
Stitches which are dropped accidentally.

EXTRA NEEDLES
Short needles pointed at both ends used to hold stitches not being knitted – sometimes called cable needles.

GRAFTING
Joining two pieces of knitting together invisibly by sewing them together with a tapestry needle – the stitches are not cast off but the loop of one stitch is sewn to the loop of another.

HEM
Fold made at the edge of knitting to stop it curling up.

HOLDING (stitches)
Stitches being held on an extra needle or a stitch holder, so that they can be knitted later. This is done when one part is to be completed before the other.

INCREASING
Adding extra stitches during knitting. There are many different methods of increasing.

JOINING TWO BALLS OF YARN
Joining the end of the first ball to the beginning of the second ball.

KNITTING IN ROUNDS
Knitting – normally on four double-pointed needles – so that the work is always turned in the same direction – thus avoiding seams.

KNITTING NEEDLES
Knitting needles can be long or short and have many different thicknesses. Long needles are necessary when there are a lot of stitches to be knitted in a row, or if you like to knit with your knitting needles tucked under your arms. The thicker the yarn the larger the diameter of the needles required.

LEAVING A STITCH
Dropping a stitch from the left-hand needle and deliberately letting it run down the rows of knitting.

LEFT-HAND SIDE
This is the left-hand side of the work when the knitting is spread out with the right side of work facing you.

NEEDLES WITHOUT KNOBS
Knitting needles pointed at both ends, usually sold in sets of 4 and used for knitting in rounds.

PICKING UP STITCHES
Taking up stitches which are not on a needle. Stitches are normally picked up from the cast-off edge or the row ends to work neck bands and front bands.

RIGHT-HAND SIDE
This is the right-hand side of the work when the knitting is spread out with the right side of work facing you

RIGHT SIDE OF WORK
The side which will be the outside of the finished garment.

ROUND
All stitches which are on the set of 4 needles when knitting in rounds.

ROW
All stitches on one needle.

SIDE EDGES
The right and left borders. There are many different methods of knitting edge stitches.

SLIP DECREASING
A method of decreasing.

SLIPPING A STITCH
Passing a stitch from the left-hand needle to the right-hand needle without knitting it.

STITCH HOLDER
A special needle for holding spare stitches – rather like a large safety pin.

STITCH PATTERN
Name given to a group of stitches forming a definite pattern.

TOGETHER
Stitches that are knitted at the same time.

Knitting knowledge

TURN
To take the right needle in the left hand and the left needle in the right hand and turn the work so that the other side is facing you.

TWISTED STITCHES
Stitches knitted by inserting the needle into the back instead of the front of the stitch.

WINDING YARN AROUND NEEDLE
Passing the yarn around the needle before knitting a stitch – normally used for lacy patterns.

WRONG SIDE OF WORK
The side which will be on the inside of the finished garment.

ABBREVIATIONS
There are many different terms and abbreviations used in knitting. Here is a list of the most important ones.

cont	=	continue
dec	=	decrease
inc	=	increase
K	=	knit plain
no.	=	number
P	=	knit purl
rem	=	remain(ing)
sl	=	slip
st(s)	=	stitch(es)
st-st	=	stocking stitch
tog	=	together

These suggestions are not rules – they are a set of common sense guide-lines that you will learn for yourself with experience. Read them and follow them and you will avoid most of the mistakes new knitters normally make.

— Always use the yarn recommended in the pattern.
— Buy sufficient yarn to complete the garment; check the ball bands all have the same dye lot number.
— If you are knitting a pattern which gives more than one size, underline the figures relating to the size you are making.
— Read the abbreviations carefully before beginning to knit and, if you are not sure of the pattern, knit a test sample.
— Keep your knitting needles in a needle case or box to avoid damaging the points.
— When knitting stripes in ribbing, knit plain the whole of the first row with the fresh colour, this will give a neater look to the ribbing.
— If you can see ridges on the wrong side of stocking stitch you are probably knitting the purl row at a tighter tension than the plain row. Try to let the yarn run a little more loosely through your fingers when purling.
— When casting off in rib on neckbands, use a size larger needle than that used for the main part of the band, and lift each stitch over the next stitch following the pattern of the ribbing. This will add extra elasticity to the neck edge.
— Follow instructions on the ball band for pressing and aftercare.

Sizes of knitting needles

Knitting needles are now sold in metric sizes. This conversion chart gives both the new international metric sizes and the old (British) sizes. As you can see with the metric sizes the higher the number, the larger the diameter of the needle, whereas with the old sizes, the higher the number the smaller the diameter.

New Metric Size	Old Size
2 mm	14
2¼mm	13
2¾mm	12
3 mm	11
3¼mm	10
3¾mm	9
4 mm	8
4½mm	7
5 mm	6
5½mm	5
6 mm	4
6½mm	3
7 mm	2
7½mm	1
8 mm	0
9 mm	00
10 mm	000

Biography

Maureen Briggs has always loved knitting and as a child designed clothes for her dolls. In 1954 she joined the knitting department of *Woman's Weekly* where she learned how to grade patterns and write knitting and crochet instructions. She has been Knitting Editor of *Woman's Weekly, Woman's Realm, Family Circle* and also of *Pins and Needles*. Now she is a freelance designer, creating knitting and crochet designs for both magazines and yarn spinners. Machine knitting is another of her interests and she owns four knitting machines! She has a teenage daughter, who is following in mother's footsteps.

Photographs

page 8   Knitting is a relaxing and useful pastime, but it's not only for grannies in rocking chairs.

12   Knitting is going metric – tape measures should have inches on one side and centimetres on the other. A basket is a useful knitting accessory.

15   Skilled shearers in Australia pride themselves on the speed with which they can remove a sheep's fleece. (Photo: International Wool Secretariat).

18   Wool being removed from a bale.

20   The scarf, the cable sweater and the Fair-Isle sweater patterns, which are illustrated in this book.

26   A stocking stitch top for summer – one of the patterns explained in this book.

31   The attractive backline of the summer top.

34   A quick-knit sweater in bold stripes – a pattern that is shown in the 'Stripey Sweaters' chapter.

38   A rare form of spinning wheel in use at Inisheer, Aran Islands Co. Galway. (Photo: Bord Failte.)

42   A sleeveless jacket with style for spring – shown in the 'Woolly Waistcoats' chapter.

45   Alternative styles on the theme of the waistcoat.

48   Draughting sheep at shearing time in Australia. (Photo: International Wool Secretariat.)

50   The blouse-on top, with simple lace bands shown in the 'Stocking Stitch Sweaters' chapter.

56   Chunky cable panels on a Stocking Stitch Sweater, shown in the 'Chunky Cable Sweaters' chapter.

61   A high speed ring wool spinning frame in action. (Photo: International Wool Secretariat.)

64   A Husky sweater with easy-to-knit coloured bands, illustrated in the chapter, 'Husky Polo Necks'.

69   The polo neck looks even better on girls, as does the jacket shown in the 'Jaunty Jackets' chapter.

72   Jaunty jacket with slit pockets.

77   Knitting garter stitch – relaxing, peaceful and productive! (Photo: Patons.)

80   This striped sweater may be stylish, but it's not accident proof!

84   The raw material – the wool from the sheep's back.